GEORG PHILIPP TELEMANN

THE 36 FANTASIAS
FOR KEYBOARD

Edited by Max Seiffert

DOVER PUBLICATIONS, INC., NEW YORK

Published in Canada by General Publishing Company, Ltd., 30 Lesmill Road, Don Mills, Toronto, Ontario.
Published in the United Kingdom by Constable and Company, Ltd.

This Dover edition, first published in 1987, contains all the music from *Drei Dutzend Klavier-Fantasien*, Verlag von Martin Breslauer, Berlin, 1923 (Vol. 4 of the Veröffentlichungen der Musik-Bibliothek Paul Hirsch, Frankfurt a. Main). A new Publisher's Note replaces the Preface of the 1923 edition.
The publisher is grateful to Queens College (Aaron Copland School of Music and Paul Klapper Library) for making this material available for direct photography.

Manufactured in the United States of America
Dover Publications, Inc., 31 East 2nd Street, Mineola, N.Y. 11501

Library of Congress Cataloging-in-Publication Data

Telemann, Georg Philipp, 1681–1767.
   [Fantaisies, harpsichord]
   The 36 fantasias for keyboard.

   Reprint. Originally published: Berlin : M. Breslauer, 1923. (Veröffentlichungen der Musik-Bibliothek Paul Hirsch ; v. 4)
   1. Harpsichord music.   I. Seiffert, Max.
M22.T33F47   1987   86-754639
ISBN 0-486-25365-1

PUBLISHER'S NOTE*

Telemann's *Fantaisies pour le clavessin; 3. Douzaines*, published by the composer in Hamburg in 1732 and 1733 in three groups of twelve (*douzaines, dozzine*), are as important historically as they are delightful aurally for performer and listener alike. Representative as they are of Telemann's introduction to Germany of the lighter and less contrapuntal *galant* style from France, these fantasias are also obvious precursors of the Classical sonata form. Some of the pieces are reminiscent of Italian chamber sonatas (two-part writing: principal voice and thoroughbass); others, of the French suite (thinly disguised dance movements); but their balanced motivic structure points ahead to the later eighteenth century. In Hamburg, specifically, they prepare the way for C. P. E. Bach.

When editing this rare collection (only two copies of the original engraved edition were known in 1923), Max Seiffert intended to offer an "Urtext." All the wording, including the page headings "Cembalo" and "Clavessin," were retained, as was the original look of the music (position of beams, use of small notes, etc.), with two important general exceptions: Seiffert printed the treble clef for the upper voice throughout the volume, and followed the modern practice of having accidentals valid for the entire measure in which they occur. He also corrected the handful of obvious engraving errors in the original directly in his text (these errors had most likely been so few because of Telemann's personal involvement in the actual engraving of the publication). Of the various repeat signs in the volume as edited, the only possibly unfamiliar one is the •/•; where this occurs in the middle of a fantasia, it instructs the player to repeat the opening rondo up to the fermata.

In his 1923 preface, Seiffert recommended (1) a discreet musical fleshing out of some of the two-part writing, especially in the middle movements of

*This note replaces the "Vorwort" written by Seiffert for the 1923 edition. The information most important for the modern user has been incorporated as part of the present Note. Most of the "Vorwort" material omitted here was a reflection of the state of Baroque music scholarship and of public awareness of Baroque composers as of 1923, a state that has been thoroughly transformed today.

the French-style fantasias, and (2) correct period ornamentation; he suggested starting trills on the upper auxiliary note, leaving it to the player to interpret each *tr* and + as a long or a short trill depending on the tempo and on note values.

Although the Italian and French wording used by Telemann is quite lucid, we offer some translations here (in the order of appearance within the volume). "Si replica la [prima] fantasia" = "Repeat the [first] fantasia." "Quinta" = "fifth." "Recommencés la [1re] fantaisie" = "Repeat the [1st] fantasia." "Voyés le commencement" = "See the beginning." "Si replica'l . . . e poi la fantasia [1]" = "Repeat the . . . and then the [first] fantasia."

The fantasias are numbered 1 through 12 in each of the three groups. The second, French, group has the page heading "Clavessin," the outer groups have "Cembalo." Each fantasia occupies two facing pages. In view of this clear organization of the book, and seeing that there are no individual titles to the pieces, it has seemed superfluous to add a table of contents or additional running heads (these elements did not exist in the 1923 edition, either).

THE 36 FANTASIAS
FOR KEYBOARD

Fantasia. *Allegro.*

Fantasia. Presto.   No. 2.

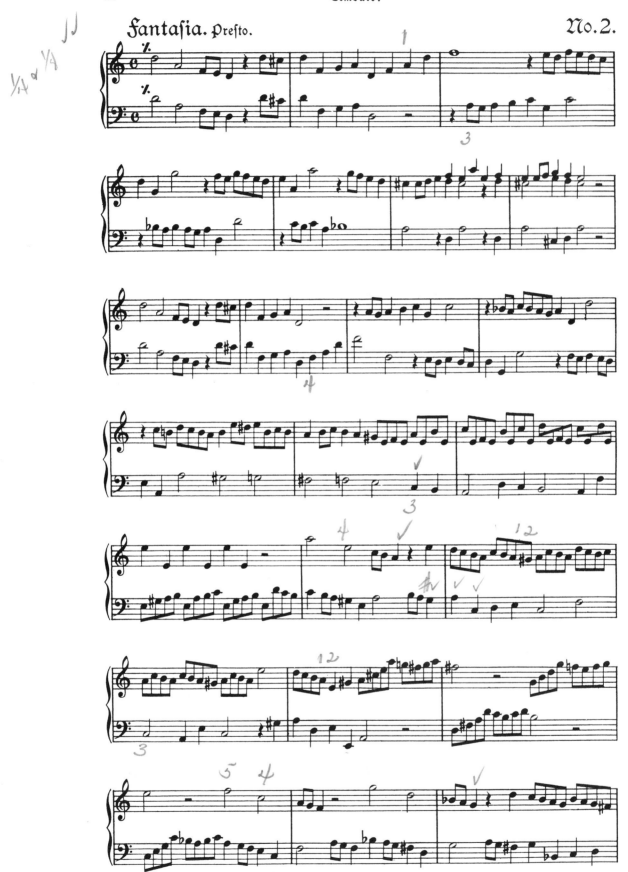

Cembalo.

Adagio.

Si replica la prima fantasia.

D.C.

Cembalo.

Fantasia. Vivace.

No. 3.

D.C.

Fantasia. Allegro.

Si replica la 3. fantasia.

D.C.

Cembalo.

Fantasia. Vivace.

No. 5.

Largo.

D.C.

Fantasia. Tempo di Minuetto.   **No. 6.**

Largo.

Si replica la quinta fantasia.

D.C.

Cembalo.

Fantasia. Presto:

No. 7.

Fantasia. *Vivace.*

No. 8.

Cantabile.

Si replica la 7. fantasia

D.C.

Fantasia. Allegro.

Cembalo.

D.C.

Fantasia. Allegro.   No. 10.

Largo.

Si replica la 9. fantasia.

D.C.

Cembalo.

Fantafia. Allegro.

No. II.

Fantasia. Vivace.

Largo.

1. Fantaiſie. Tendrement.   2. Douzaine.

Tendrement;
voyés le
commencement.

Tres vîte.

2. Fantaisie. Gravement.

Gayment.

Allegrement.

Gravement;
voyés le
commencement.

recommencés la 1ʳᵉ fantaisie.

3. Fantaiſie. Pompeuſement.　　　　　　　　　　2. Douzaine.

Pompeuſement;
voyés le
commencement

Gayment.

4. Fantaiſie. Gratieuſement.

Vivement.

Gratieuſement;
voyés le
commencement.

Vîte.

recommencés la 3me fantaiſie.

5. Fantaisie. Melodieusement.　　　　　　　　　　2. Douzaine.

Spirituellement.

Melodieuſement;
voyés le
commencement.

Vîte.

6. Fantaisie. Tendrement.

Gayment.

Tendrement;
voyés le
commencement.

Vîte.

recommencés la 5me fantaisie.

7. **Fantaisie.** Lentement.

2. Douzaine.

Allegrement.

Lentement;
voyés le
commencement.

Vivement.

8. Fantaisie. Gratieusement.   2. Douzaine.

Gratieuſement;
voyés le
commencement:

Gayment.

recommencés la 7me fantaiſie.

9. Fantaiſie. Flateuſement.

Vivement.

Flateusement;
voyés le
commencement.

Tres vîte.

10. Fantaiſie. Moderement.

Vivement.

Moderement;
voyés le
commencement.

Gayment.

recommencés la 9. fantaisie.

11. Fantaisie. Pompeusement.

Allegrement.

Pompeuſement;
voyés le
commencement.

Vite.

12. **Fantaiſie.** Gratieuſement.   2. Douzaine.

Gratieuſement;
voyés le
commencement.

Vitement.

recommencés la 11. fantaiſie.

Fantafia I. *Vivace.*

Si replica'l
Divace.

Fantasia 2. Vivace.

Si replica'l Vivace, e poi la fantasia I.

Fantasia 3. Tempo giusto

Presto.

Si replica'l tempo giusto.

Fantasia 4. Vivace.

Dolce.

Si replica 'l Vivace, e poi la fantasia 3.

Fantasia 5. Allegro. Cembalo. Dozzina 3.

Si replica'l Allegro.

Fantaſia 6. Gratioſo.

Vivace.

Si replica 'l gratioso, e poi la fantasia 5.

Fantasia 7. Presto.

Arioso.

Si replica 'l
presto.

Cembalo.

Fantasia 8. Vivace.

Minue.

Si replica 'l vivace, e poi la fantasia 7.

Fantasia 9. Allegro.

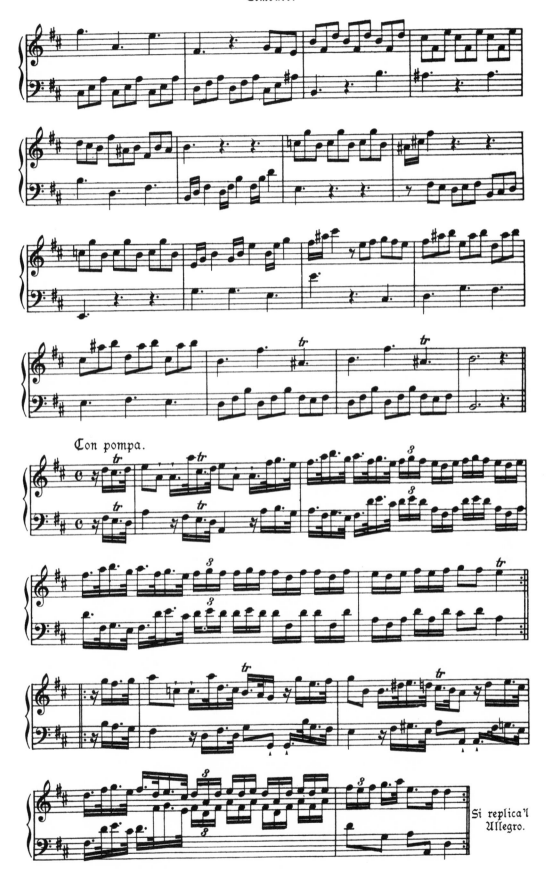

Con pompa.

Si replica'l
Allegro.

Fantasia 10. Allegro.

Si replica'l allegro, e poi la fantasia 9.

Fantasia II. *Vivace.* Dozzina 3.